St. Ives through the Victorian Magic Lantern

At the end of the 19th century, there was a yearning for times past, when England's towns and cities were unpolluted by belching factory chimneys and the pace of life was slower. Some of the best Victorian photographers took and sold photographs which reflected this pre-industrial, perceived 'golden age' and the visual charm of St. Ives provided suitable locations and subjects. Over one hundred years later, these photographs enable us to step back in time and experience fragmentary moments in the lives of our Victorian ancestors.

This booklet reproduces photographs of St. Ives from the Keasbury-Gordon Photograph Archive. Most of them were taken by Graystone Bird who won many awards for his photography but is now virtually unknown because of the 'forgotten' format in which his images were published, glass 'magic lantern' projection slides. The photos of Pilchard fishermen were taken by an amateur photographer in south west Cornwall but the precise location is unknown. The text is from a travel guide which was published in 1898. It is in two parts, a history and general description of Cornwall and a detailed exploration of the area around St. Ives. The map is from the same book.

The photographs and the text complement each other and enable us to travel back in time to visit this delightful corner of Victorian England. I hope you enjoy the journey.

The magic lantern was the predecessor of the pre-digital slide projector. The first magic lanterns were made in the mid-1600s by natural philosophers (early scientists) who were exploring the nature and commercial potential of optics. Light sources and lenses improved throughout the 1700s and 1800s and, as a consequence, it was possible to show bigger, brighter and clearer pictures to ever larger audiences. During Queen Victoria's reign, magic lantern shows became established as mass-media entertainment. Shows could be lavish, theatrical events with all the razzmatazz of today's TV talent contests, with multiple lanterns to produce special effects. Magic lanterns were also used in Church and village halls and educational establishments for talks and lectures and, of course, in ordinary homes for family entertainment.

Some slides gave the illusion of movement. These included colourful kaleidoscopes, children skipping, a dentist pulling teeth and a man swallowing rats as he sleeps with his mouth open ...... still a favourite with children (of all ages) who attend my magic lantern shows.

In the early 1800s, magic lanterns were used to create phantasmagoria horror shows, where terrifying devils, witches and the grim reaper were conjured out of thin air, with accompanying sound effects, in suitably scary venues. These shows employed the latest technology and created sophisticated illusions to entice customers to part with their money and be scared out of their wits.

Magic lantern slides were made of glass. Early ones were hand painted and expensive to produce and buy but, from the mid 1800s, photographic images were applied to slides, mass-production followed and the magic lantern industry boomed. In its heyday, the 1890s, millions of slides were made, particularly in Britain, France and America, for entertainment, amusement, education, spiritual enlightenment and moral crusades.

In Britain, manufacturers of lantern slides produced sales catalogues of individual and sets of slides that could be purchased or hired by mail-order or from local, high-street outlets. Photographic slides produced by Graystone Bird were critically acclaimed then and much admired by collectors now.

Graystone Bird was born in Somerset in 1862. His father, Frederick Charles Bird, ran a successful photographic business in Frome and in 1866 opened a new studio in Milsom Street, Bath. Around the age of fifteen, Graystone was apprenticed to his father to learn the technicalities of photography and the skills necessary for him to inherit the family business, the core of which was portrait photography. By the early 1890s, the business was producing a growing range of magic lantern slides, from photographs taken by Graystone. By 1896 he had succeeded his father as the proprietor of the business. He was an astute businessman and as well as selling photographs direct to the public from the Milsom Street shop and by mail-order, he also licensed other slide producers to use his images. Graystone promoted his business by attending photographic exhibitions. He won over two hundred prizes for individual photographs, including awards from international exhibitions in Vienna and Chicago and his work was recognised in America, Canada, Australia and Switzerland.

Graystone's slides are instantly recognisable by their unique style. They are very sharp with fine tone and contrast and often include people in artistic poses. Today, they form an important historical record of life in the communities that he photographed including Whitby, the Isle of Man, Castle Combe in Wiltshire and St. Ives and Newlyn. He died in 1943.

ST. IVES AND PENZANCE

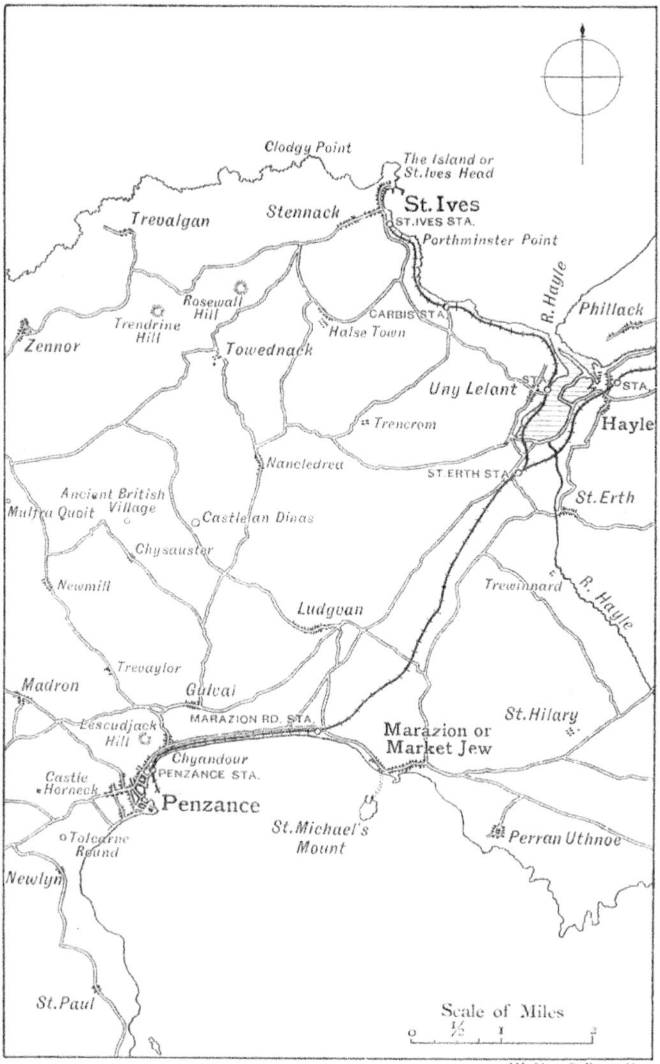

Walker & Boutall sc.

Tin Mines from Rosewall Hill

The Hayle Lifeboat

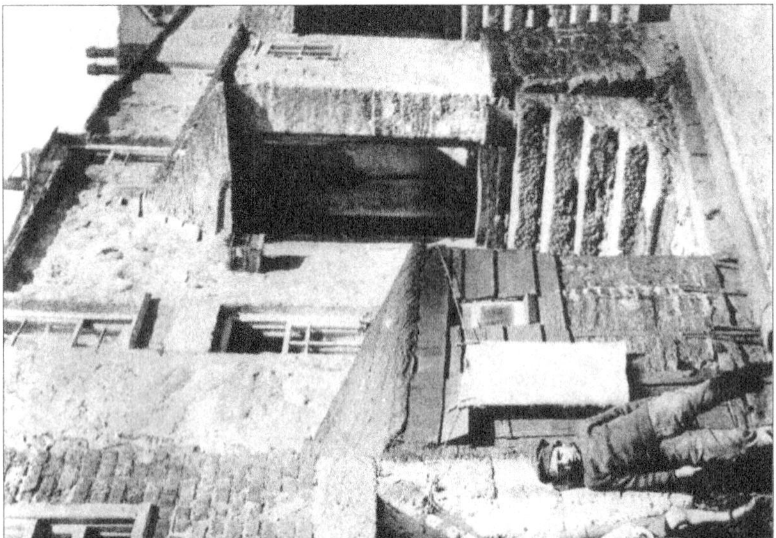

SS 537

PHOTOGRAPHIC ESTABLISHMENT

Pilchard fishing using a seine net (above and below)

Pilchard fishing using a seine net (above and below)

INTRODUCTION

The "Duchy of Cornwall," as this south-western appendix of England loves to be styled, is a country of markedly individual characteristics, distinguishing it from all other parts of the kingdom. Many strangers crossing the Tamar, "over that fairy bridge of Brunel's, hung aloft between the blue of the river and the blue of the sky," are fain to fancy themselves in another country; and as they advance, it is to find that impression deepened which gives a Cornish tour something of the interest of foreign travel. Truth to tell, this interest is mainly confined to the broken and wave-beaten coast-line, almost uniformly striking, and often magnificent, broken by frequent fishing havens that to more than one sense suggest the kind of picturesqueness looked for under a Mediterranean sky. Inland, the scenery, dear as it may be to those who have known it from childhood, is apt to affect the unfamiliar eye as dreary in its monotonous expanse of rough brown moors, swelling up into low ridges, scarred by mines and topped by smokeless engine-shafts to take the place of trees—"a most unclassical Campagna, covered with the ruins of obscure industry." Even the dignity of height is wanting here, Brown Willy, the loftiest point in Cornwall, being under 1400 feet.

Cornwall's jovial neighbours are in the way of asserting that it does not grow wood enough to make a coffin. This of course is a calumny; but timber here has to be sought for in the sheltered hollows, often nourishing a thick growth of oak-coppice, as well as statelier trees, among them the small-leaved Cornish elm, so rarely found in other counties. On the open heights, flowering its best at that season when, as poets tell us, kissing comes most in favour, glows a profusion of gorse, including the double-blossomed sort, which, with the various heaths, the white *erica vagans* and the *ciliaris* their peculiar pride, and the splendid cliff-carpeting of the sea pink, the hardy bloom of brambles, and the graceful verdure of tamarisks in warm nooks, as well as the stains of lichen upon hoary rocks, themselves often finely tinted, go far to relieve the prevailing dulness of colour. Brick appears rarely where its becoming background of green is wanting; but whitewash is much used, with lively effect, on the open landscapes. The stair-like Cornish stiles, the substantial walls and hedges, the conical "windmow" stacks, the prominence of church towers and other beacon marks, are striking features on the face of the country.

The time when Cornwall is seen to the best advantage is perhaps in spring, which here comes to meet one from the Atlantic; or in late autumn, while a hectic glow still lingers about "the good gigantic smile o' the old brown earth." Those who love the "high midsummer pomps" might feast their eyes more fully elsewhere. In winter this scenery suffers less than that of most other parts. As the question of weather is a most important one to tourists, we will begin with it in sketching the qualities of a district which gets more than its fair share of what wind and rain are going in our island.

The **Climate** of Cornwall is the most equable on the British mainland, owing to the manner in which this tongue of land, almost surrounded by sea, is washed by the Gulf Stream and brushed by the prevalent south-west winds. The southern end, less exposed to other influences, is remarkably mild in winter and not often hot in summer, the usual range of temperature being about 20°. Snow and frost seldom hold out long against the mild breath of the Atlantic; yet, now and again natives are surprised and strangers disappointed by a visitation of exceptional severity, as in the spring blizzard of 1891 and the long hard winter of 1895. Such a climate has the defects of its qualities; it takes all the bracing force of sea air to save it from being relaxing in its humid softness, which, indeed, seems not to hurt the health of those born under its mists and clouds. Tourists, taking one month with another, must reckon at least every second day as likely to be more or less wet, and will be lucky not to come in now and then for a week of rain; but all the more clear and lovely are the glimpses of sunshine, for which, in winter, Cornwall has a good chance of being better off than its neighbours. As hinted above, the sea winds prevent timber trees from reaching any great size in open situations; but lower growths show singular luxuriance in sheltered nooks, especially of the south coast. About Falmouth and Penzance, and in the Scilly Isles, several varieties of palms, cacti, and camellias, and other exotics flourish under the open air. The olive tree has been planted with success in a few places. The Austrian pine, and other foreigners of this species, do well in the western parts. Stone fruit, however, and apples and pears, do not generally gain the same full flavour as in Devon, for want of dry heat.

Geology.—The Carbonaceous formations of North Devon extend into the north-western angle of the county, but by far the greater part of Cornwall belongs to the Devonian or greywacke series of rocks, consisting of slates and shales, which occupy much of South Devon, and occur again in North Devon and Somersetshire. From the Devonians four large patches of granite project at intervals. The Land's End district forms the most westerly of these granite patches. A large mass of serpentine occupies the district about the Lizard Head; and the Devonian rocks are traversed by numerous veins and outbreaks of trap and of "elvan,"—the name locally given to porphyries, granitic and felspathic. But to a great extent the cliffs are of slate, taking on a grimly bristling roughness under the lashing of the waves, especially along the storm-beaten walls of the north-west coast-line.

INTRODUCTION

Of the mineral veins, for which Cornwall has so long been famous, tin is found in both granite and slate ; copper for the most part in granite. The most important Cornish copper ore is the sulphuret, commonly known as grey ore by the miners ; but copper pyrites, or the bisulphuret of copper, occurs far more frequently in both Cornwall and Devon. The tin of Cornwall has been known and worked from a period long before the dawn of certain history. Copper, which lies deeper in the earth, and consequently cannot be "streamed" for, was almost unnoticed in the county until the end of the 15th century, and little attention was paid to it until the last years of the 17th. No mine seems to have been worked exclusively for copper before the year 1700 ; soon after which a Mr. Coster gave great impulse to the industry by draining some of the deeper mines, and instructing the men in an improved method of dressing the ore.

Unfortunately, the Cornish mines have been steadily decaying in value of late years. In every sense they are going down, and the deeper the workings the more expensive it becomes to bring up the metal, while in other parts of the world their rivals are in the position of our early miners, who got their easy gains near the surface. For the tin trade, Cornwall finds its chief competitor in the Straits Settlements, where the mineral is abundant and the labour cheap. As there, moreover, payments are received in gold, and expenses mainly paid in depreciated silver, the vexed controversy of bimetallism comes in to trouble the heads of Cornish village politicians. Another much disputed question is as to attracting outside capital by making the mines into Limited Liability Companies. At present most of them are mainly owned in the neighbourhood, and often in small shares, which spread the interest in their prosperity and give honest Cornishmen something of the excitement without the guilt of gambling. This diffused speculation is quite a feature of the local character ; it has been said that nearly every Cornishman feels certain of being descended from King Arthur and of being destined to make his fortune in a mine, as so many have done before him. Fortunes are not made in mines nowadays; and, as one and the other comes to be "knacked," the loss is at once felt in the locality, both directly and indirectly. Copper is even in a worse plight than tin. The only industries of the kind doing at all well at present are the granite quarries, and the china clay workings in the centre of the county. The fisheries, too, that second string to Cornwall's bow, are not what they once were. A people singularly attached to their own soil, find themselves, then, more and more obliged to emigrate. Cornish miners turn up all over the world, now in South America, helping to ruin their old country, now behind the walls of Lucknow, throwing down the musket for the pick and recalling their old trade to baffle the sapping of the wily sepoy. Thus the population has been steadily thinning, till at the last census it numbered less than 318,600, over an area of nearly 1350 square miles, a decrease of 50,000 in one generation. In the mining districts, where this population groups thickest, it is drawn into clusters which here and there run together without rounding themselves off with municipal dignity, unless they go to swell some former nucleus of intercourse. No town in Cornwall contains more than about 15,000 inhabitants; and even then this figure is reached by counting in straggling suburbs that can hardly be distinguished from large independent villages. On purely agricultural land, the population is more dissemin-ated, as on the coast, where, however, it gathers every few miles into snug fishing villages, while the "church town" of large moorland parishes may be a mere hamlet.

The Geology of Cornwall has thus had such an influence on its progress that we are led into considerations which might appropriately have followed a sketch of its history, when we pass to man from nature.

History.—Cornwall, like the rest of England, is first found inhabited by a Celtic race, who may here have supplanted a still older stock. In such a familiar feature as the saffron with which Cornishmen still love to colour their cakes, enthusiastic antiquaries have seen a touch of early

Oriental intercourse; but we have no authentic knowledge of this country until after the Roman conquest of Britain. It remains uncertain whether Phœnician or Carthaginian traders actually visited the "Cassiterides," or whether they obtained their supplies of tin through Gaul. But we know that the tin of the district was largely exported from a very early period, and that the mines were still worked under the Romans. Cornwall formed part of the British Kingdom of Damnonia, which long resisted the advance of the Saxons westward, and remained almost unbroken in power until the reign of Ine of Wessex (688-726). From that time the borders of the British Kingdom gradually narrowed, until, about the year 926, Athelstan drove the Britons from Exeter, and fixed the Tamar as the limit between them and the Saxons of Devon. So at least say some authorities, while others place the boundary on a line between Plymouth and Tintagel, and reduce Athelstan's exploit to driving back a fresh Celtic irruption, perhaps made in alliance with the Danes. The British bishop, Conan, submitted to Archbishop Wulfhelm of Canterbury after Athelstan's conquest, and was reappointed by him in 936. The Cornish see was afterwards merged in that of Crediton, then in 1050 the place of the united sees was transferred to Exeter, where it remained till 1876. Cornwall, although the mass of the people remained Celtic, speedily received Saxon masters, and in the Domesday Survey the recorded names of the owners of land are all Saxon. The Conqueror bestowed nearly the whole county on his half-brother, Robert of Mortain, and thus arose the Earldom of Cornwall, which, considered too important a possession to be held by any one under royal rank, came to be an appanage of the heir-apparent to the crown. In 1336 the earldom was raised to a Duchy by Edward III. in favour of his son, the Black Prince, and of his heirs, eldest sons of the Kings of England. Since that time the Prince of Wales has always been Duke of Cornwall. The Duchy originally included Dartmoor Forest; and its income is at present derived from lands in Somerset and Devon as well as in Cornwall itself. The history of the Duchy is virtually that of Cornwall. There has been little to connect it with the general annals of the country except for rebellions under the Tudors, and during the Civil War, when Cornwall was for the most part royalist. Besides much skirmishing, there were two important battles within its bounds, that of Braddock Down (Jan. 19, 1642-3), and that of Stratton (May 15, 1643), both gained for the King. The more important histories of the county embrace Carew's *Survey of Cornwall*, Drew's *History of Cornwall*, Hal's *Parochial History of Cornwall*, Polwhele's *History of Cornwall*. Among recent works on the subject are Daniell and Collins's *History of Cornwall*, the *Church History of Cornwall*, and the *Parochial History* published by Mr. Lake.

Antiquities.—No part of England preserves so many antiquities of the primæval period. These chiefly abound in the district between Penzance and the Land's End, but they occur in all the wilder parts of the county. They may be classed as follows:—(1) *Cromlechs*. These in the west of Cornwall are called "quoits," with a reference to their broad and flat covering stones. The largest and most important are those known as Lanyon, Caerwynen, Mulfra, Chun, and Zennor quoits, all in the Land's End district. Of these Chun is the only one which has not been thrown down. Zennor is said to be the largest in the British Isles, while Lanyon, when perfect, was of sufficient height for a man on horseback to ride under. Of those in the eastern part of Cornwall, Trethevy near Liskeard and Pawton in the parish of St. Breock are the finest, and have remained intact. (2) Rude uninscribed *monoliths* are common to all parts of Cornwall. Those at Boleit, in the parish of Buryan, are perhaps the most important. (3) *Circles*, none of which are of great dimensions. The principal are the Hurlers, near Liskeard; the Boskednan, Boscawen-un, and Tregeseal circles; and that called the Dawns-un, or Merry Maidens. All of these, except the Hurlers, are in the Land's End district. Other circles that may be mentioned are the "Trippet Stones," in the Parish of Blisland, and one at Duloe.

(4) Long *alignments* or *avenues* of stones, resembling those on Dartmoor, but not so perfect, are to be found on the moors near Roughtor and Brown Willy. A very remarkable monument of this kind exists in the neighbourhood of St. Columb, called the "Nine Maidens." It consists of nine rude pillars placed in a line, while near them is a single stone known as the "Old Man." (5) *Hut dwellings.* Of these there are at least two kinds, those in the eastern part of the county resembling the beehive structures and enclosures of Dartmoor, and those in the west, comprising "hut-clusters," having a central court, and a surrounding wall often of considerable height and thickness. The bee-hive masonry is also found in connection with these latter, as are also (6) *Caves,* or subterraneous structures, resembling those of Scotland and Ireland. (7) *Cliff castles* are a characteristic feature of the Cornish coast, as for example the "Little Dinas" near Falmouth, Trevalgue, near St. Columb, and Treryn, Mên, Kenidjack, Bosigran, and others in the west. These are all fortified against the land side. (8) *Hill castles,* or camps, are very numerous. Castle-an-Dinas, near St. Columb, is the best example of the earthwork camp, and Chun Castle, near Penzance, of the stone.

One of the most difficult problems of British archæology is to fix the epoch and race to which these prehistoric remains belong. The old theory of the days of Dr. Borlase and his followers, that they are Druidical, is now obsolete. The tendency of modern research is to throw their date back into a remote past long anterior to Julius Cæsar's conquest of Britain and the Christian era. Possibly they belong to an age before the arrival of even the Celts into Western Europe.

Of early Christian and mediæval antiquities the most noticeable are crosses, scattered all over the county, and of various dates, from the 6th to the 16th century, many resembling the early crosses of Wales; inscribed sepulchral stones of the 7th and 8th centuries, of which the "Mên scryffa" in Madron is a good example; and oratories of the Early Irish type like St. Pirans. This county is particularly well off for holy wells, whose wonder-working virtues are still not forgotten by a half-believing, half-jesting generation; and beside these wells are often found the ruins of ancient baptisteries consecrated by the shadowy memory of some saint.

It is well known how rich Cornwall was in local saints—St. Piran, St. Nectan, St. Morwenna, St. Juliot, St. Eval, St. Ervyn, and countless others, whose names are hardly met with beyond its border. Almost every letter of the alphabet forms an initial in the peculiar nomenclature of Cornish parishes. The churches, for the most part, belong to the Perpendicular style, and show a simplicity in keeping with their surroundings. They are generally low in the body, but with high and plain granite towers. The rich tower of Probus, however, is an exception, and that of St. Austell, as well as the Church of St. Mary Magdalene at Launceston, the exterior of which is covered with sculpture. A peculiar feature found in several instances is a campanile or separated belfry. Within, the chief local characteristic is the absence of a chancel arch.

The castles of Launceston, Trematon, and Restormel seem to be of the time of Henry III., but the mounds which occur in the first two are no doubt much earlier,—possibly marking British strongholds. Tintagel has but a few shapeless walls. St. Michael's Mount, although castellated at an early period, has nothing more ancient than the 15th century. Pendennis, Star Fort, and others, are of Tudor date.

Language.—Of the Celtic tongues, Cornish and Armoric (the dialect of Brittany in France) resembled each other more than either of them did Welsh, nor is this the only trace of a connection which geographical situation has made natural.

The literary remains are very scanty. The old Cornish language was spoken till the 18th century, still surviving in a few fishing and mining terms, as in names of persons and places, "Pol, Tre, and Pen." The last sentence of the language used by the fishermen of Mount's Bay seems to have been "*Breal meta truja peswartha*—all is scrawed all along the line O." This mixed Cornish and English was used in living memory. The numerals (also remembered by a few in Newlyn and Mousehole) are :—

1. Un.	4. Padzher.	8. Eith.
2. Du.	5. Pemp.	9. Nau.
3. Tri.	6. Wheth.	10. Deig.
	7. Seith.	

The Cornish of our day are a mixed race, mainly Celtic, well made and sturdy in form. As in Ireland, the aristocracy has been largely of Norman or Saxon origin ; but these grafts have quickly taken the qualities of the old stock ; and here, as in Ireland, there seems something in the soil or the air to make intruders soon become *Cornubiensibus Cornubiensiores.* For Cornishmen are strongly marked by clannishness of an even more accentuated type than that found in west-countrymen generally, and seem to regard their fellow-subjects over the Tamar almost as foreigners. "Going to England" is the phrase with one who leaves his native county. The character of the people has been strongly tempered by the exciting pursuits of mining and fishing, not to speak of smuggling and wrecking practices that held out here after civilisation had tamed the lawless instincts of their neighbours. Even in this century the inhabitants of the Cornish coast proved hard to teach that a wreck was not fair game ; and dark stories are told of how a ship would actually be enticed unto destruction on this cruel shore, that human vultures might gather to her plunder. The grandsons of those wreckers now man the lifeboats ; yet something of the old Adam still seems to run in their blood, for it is said that a Cornishman will work harder and for less wages upon a wreck than at any other job. A rough population it must have been among whom John Wesley came, and found here an arena for an inspiring struggle with the devil. The results of his labours are well known ; probably the hottest Churchman will admit that Methodism has been a regenerating force, through which a people not easily tamed have become remarkably sober and orderly. Other forms of dissent flourish, notably the Bryanite or Bible Christian sect, which has its stronghold in this corner of the country. On the other hand, the Established clergy, by a natural movement of repulsion, are apt to lean towards the High Church side. It should be said that an imaginative temperament gives a strong tinge of superstition to Cornish religion ; but stirring devotion here seems to have a wholesomely practical effect.

One point may be confidently insisted on : if Cornish clannishness is quick to resent the intrusion of outsiders in business, the idle stranger may be assured of friendly civility. His Celtic blood, and his independent pride, make every Cornishman more or less a gentleman ; so there is no part of England where the manners of all classes leave so little to be desired. We have used the word civility ; but that poorly expresses the hearty kindliness with which a visitor will find himself welcomed and furthered, so long as he remember not to abuse goodwill, to despise well-meant efforts, or to insult prejudice. Few who make their holiday quarters in Cornwall but come back with a warm memory of the honest solicitude of some motherly hostess, the untutored courtesy of some boatman, the rough willingness of some miner or labourer who has turned aside to help the bewildered wayfarer. Here indeed it seems that—

> "Stranger is a holy name ;
> Rest and a guide, and food and fire,
> In vain he never must require."

While the temptation of gain, and continued commerce with those who place the heart in the purse, have done something to sophisticate some Cornwall hostelries, there are others where one is amazed that so little advantage is taken of opportunity to tax a visitor for entertainment offered as if "all for love and nothing for reward." And if some of these lodgings for travellers be not over-luxurious in their accommodations, we have good authority for holding that better is a dinner of tough fowls and plainly cooked herbs, under certain circumstances, than a *table d'hôte* menu and a host of Swiss waiters whose attentions become overpowering at the moment of payment. One who can fare on Cornish cream and Cornish cakes will find himself always at home here, nor, if his coming be expected, will he go without more solid repasture. But should his lot be cast in farm or cottage, a tender soul must harden himself against the draughts of fresh air likely to be freely supplied at most seasons of the year.

The backbone of travelling in this county is the Great Western Railway, which runs from Plymouth to Penzance, with branches to the narrow limits on either side. In the north part its rival, the London and South-Western Company, has taken an inch that may before long become an ell. The adventurous Cornishmen were early in welcoming railways with Celtic impulsiveness, but had not always counted the cost with Saxon prudence, so some side lines will be seen lying idle, overgrown with rust and grass, and others that are used only for the conveyance of minerals. The diffused grouping of the population leads to the railway communication being supplemented by many local coaches, omnibuses, and queer caravans, most of which find no place in imperial time-tables, but might often prove helpful to the leisurely traveller. The cyclist need not fear to be often brought to a stand here, though he must duly beware of abrupt steeps and rugged moorland tracks. One way or other the tourist will have little difficulty in getting about Cornwall; but this is a county the best points of which cannot be so well seen as by the pilgrim who with staff and scrip—not to say waterproof and stoutish sandals—fares sturdily on foot. To "One and all," as the Cornish motto has it, we wish *bon voyage;* and, we hope, have done our best to make the wish no idle compliment.

ST. IVES.

We now come to deal with the peninsula of **Penwith**, of which *St. Ives* is the capital on the north, and *Penzance* on the south. At *St. Erth Junction* goes off the short branch to *St. Ives* (4 m.). Here, if desired, the guard would telegraph for quarters or omnibus to the principal St. Ives Hotel, which belongs to the G.W.R. Co., and stands out of the town. The stations on the way are *Lelant* and *Carbis Bay*, which some day may come to be called suburbs of St. Ives. On the right of the line are pleasant views, first of the *Hayle River* Estuary and the towans beyond, then of the open Bay.

ST. IVES.

Hotels.—*Tregenna Castle*, in its own grounds, above the town; *Porthminster Hotel*, above the station.

The other hostelries, *Western, Queen's, White Hart*, etc., in the town, are what our *confrère* Baedeker would call "unpretending," more or less.

The railway lands us below the elevated quarter of St. Ives known as *Porthminster*, where the best of the new houses have been built. From the "Terrace" here, and the "Malakoff" bastion at the corner, there is a fine view over the bay to *Godevery Island* with its lighthouse, *St. Agnes Head* beyond, and *Trevose Head* sometimes descried in the far distance; then, to the other side, upon the old town thickly huddled together at the neck of the peninsula called the "Island," so as to suggest, in miniature, the situation of Llandudno below its Great Orme's Head. The rocks here are not particularly bold or striking, and beyond the Hayle river the coast-line is made up of barren "towans," falling away into a featureless shore; but the sweep of the bay is very graceful, and the colouring of the water often imitates the brilliant hues of the Mediterranean.

Descending the road from the Terrace, or taking the shore walk below the station, we soon reach the stately Church tower (120 feet) that marks the heart of the town. A good specimen of a true Cornish church, though of unusual breadth, containing, besides two aisles, a half-aisle or "Trenwith Chapel," it stands so close to the sea that in rough weather the east windows are washed by the spray. Several of the windows are filled with modern glass; that representing *Faith, Hope, and Charity*, to the right of the entrance, is very fine, though in the comparative sobriety of its tints it may not be the first to strike the inartistic eye. This church is specially rich in old oak carvings on the pulpit, the bench ends under the tower, and those of the Trenwith aisle, and the front of the choir, which are said to have been the work of a blacksmith, and bear among their devices the emblems of his trade. The waggon roof, the pavement, the Norman font, and several monuments to local families are also noteworthy.

From the church we pass out into the little cramped market-place, round which are grouped some very quaint old buildings. Into it leads, on one hand, a small bit of High Street, and at right angles to this, on the other side, Fore Street, where the Post Office is, and which, skirting the harbour, forms the longest and straightest thoroughfare. All around branch off obscure openings into that labyrinth of narrow, crooked, dark, roughly-paved streets, alleys, courts, stairways, what in Scotland would be called "closes," and other feats of crowded domestic architecture, which make St. Ives almost unique among English towns. One element of the picturesque, as presented in Catholic countries, is not wanting here—an ancient and fish-like smell, which might convert the most determined enemy of tobacco, where the explorer must often hold his nose, as well as stoop his head and look to his feet. The names of some of these nooks are as singular as their aspect—*the Digey*, *Puddingbag Lane*, *Chy-an-Chy*, *Street-an-Garrow*, *Bunkers' Hill* will serve as examples. In spite of smells, this close-packed town has hitherto been very healthy, while defying, in its former want of sanitary appliances, all the theories of science, and still flying in the face of *fin-de-siècle* notions of decency by the practice of some old inhabitants. It is to be hoped that modern sewerage will be carried out thoroughly, so as to give no handle of reproach to *laudatores temporis acti*. The strength and stature of the population, indeed, is said to have suffered from frequent intermarriages, though in past days there has been an infusion of Spanish and other outlandish blood, as may be guessed by the foreign type of some faces that would not strike one as strange at Bordeaux or at Cadiz.

From the harbour we pass on to the rocky slopes of the Island, blackened with nets spread out to dry. This has been an actual island, like the whole peninsula now joined to the mainland by the Hayle Sands. Upon the promontory, which thus forms an epitome of Penwith, we find a little house, once *St. Nicholas' Chapel*, and traces of ancient British fortification, besides a dismantled battery at the point, where we get a view over the sands of Porthminster and of Porthmeor Bays on either hand, sometimes bristling with the skeleton of some shipwrecked hull embedded here. The waves of a south-west gale dashing against this point must make a fine spectacle.

The rising ground behind the Island is fast covering itself with new houses, which make up for what they want in picturesque squalor by more light and air, and a better supply of modern conveniences. Here lodgings may be looked for ; but the most genteel quarter seems to be that farther east, above the station.

St. Ives at one time held a much more important position among the towns of the west, and is fortunate in having its history set forth with unusual minuteness in a goodly volume by Mr. J. H. Matthews, as he was in finding rarely full materials to work upon. The borough accounts and records from A.D. 1639 to 1776 had been available, when in 1890 a tattered bundle of papers was discovered by accident, which, carefully examined and restored, proved to be an earlier volume, carrying the municipal archives back to 1570. These records, largely drawn on by Mr. Matthews, are a treasure of side-lights into the political and social life of two vanished centuries, and help us vividly to realise the troubles and pastimes of St. Ives citizens. From first to last there is a great paying out for drink and other refreshments, 4s. now being expended for beer at the beating of the parish bounds, and four times as much being again laid out at the tavern upon "our Recorder and other gents." Parsons coming to preach are treated to wine, and shipwrecked sailors and strangers, one is glad to know, are sent on their way not without provision. Beer given the ringers at the proclamation of the Lord Protector cost 10s. ; but on Charles II.'s coronation it flowed in barrelfuls to more than ten times that amount. Sixpence was paid for "whipping a thief," and as much for administering the same salutary discipline to a "maid that would drown herself." Whipping of such offenders, and mending of the stocks, cage, and pillory are frequent items of expense. One shilling was spent on beating the parish bounds into the fickle memory of boys, who in those days were thought never the worse of chastisement; while it cost £1 : 2s. "taking the Quakers to Launceston" to jail there, George Fox among them probably, whose descendants, by the whirligig of time, now fill such a respected place in this country. "Amending the drum" also figures more than once in the municipal accounts, which, on such occasions as the king's birthday, record lavish expenditure on drummers, fiddlers, and the like. We have picked out some of the more trivial of these extracts, which abound both in instruction and amusement. But St. Ives has some grim records, as that of its rebel Portreeve hanged in the Market Place on a gallows prepared while he was entertaining the king's commissioner at dinner.

To our own century belongs the diary of a local Pepys, one John T. Short, a manuscript, still extant, that provides us with a remarkable abstract and brief chronicle of his time, dealing with small matters as well as great. This diary is likely to be published in full in the *St. Ives Summary*, one of the smallest of weekly papers, which has already given to the world reminiscences by the same writer of his adventures as a prisoner of war in France. A similar story of captivity by another St. Ives man, Thomas Williams, has also been published in its columns, and in Mr. Matthews' *History*.

These artless narratives remind us how St. Ives has known the pains of war, and taken its share in manning the wooden walls of Old England. At the present day its harbour makes a good port of refuge on a coast very ill off for safe havens; and a score or more vessels will sometimes take shelter here in rough weather. St. Ives has a locally-owned line of steamers whose names all begin with *Tre*, as Truro sends forth a fleet in *Pen*; but we fancy Cardiff to be their chief port of departure. The office of this Company, a remarkable Georgian mansion, should be noticed in the centre of the town. For long its chief maritime concern has been with the pilchard fishery, of which it may be considered as the headquarters, though perhaps surpassed in number of boats and men by the fishing villages of Mount's Bay.

Pilchard Fishery.—The pilchard, though not very different in size and other respects from a herring or from a large sardine, is almost peculiar to the Cornwall coast, living habitually in deep water not far west of the Scilly Isles, and visiting the coast in great shoals. Twelve millions of pilchards are said to have been taken in a single day ; and the indications of such a great army of fish passing the Land's End, pursued by hordes of dog-fish, hake, and cod, besides vast flocks of sea-birds, is the buried treasure of a St. Ives boy's dream. When brought to shore the pilchards are carried to the cellars to be cured. They are then packed in hogsheads, each containing about 2400 fish. These casks are largely exported to Naples and other Italian ports—whence the fishermen's toast, "Long life to the Pope, and death to thousands !" Spanish customers, from a mistaken idea of their being smoked, called them *fumados*, hence the Cornish name "fair maids."

The pilchards are expected off the coast in October, when their appearance gives rise to general excitement at a place like St. Ives. Often have been described the patient watching of the *huers* on the cliffs, who with a huge trumpet at length announce their joyful discovery, and by the waving of bushes telegraph the movements of the shoal marked by the colour of the sea and its hovering escort of gulls ; the rush of men, women, and children to the shore with shouts of *heva! heva!* which is Cornish for the classic *Eureka;* the marshalling of the seine boats ; the shooting of the huge nets ; the enclosure of the luckless victims by myriads ; then the hurried orgy of capturing, pickling and storing, stimulated by its promise of prosperity to the whole place.

These exciting scenes have been to some extent superseded by what is really the old method of drift-net fishing, where the boats, by night, go out farther to sea to meet their prey, and the incidents are not so dramatic if the results prove more satisfactory. The drift fishing is accused by some old people of frightening away the pilchards from less fortunately placed stations, perhaps on the same principle as Tenterden Steeple was the cause of Goodwin Sands. It is certain that they no longer favour parts of the coast where once their yearly coming brought no small gain. The manner of curing also has changed, the old way of drysalting having given place to pickling in tanks of brine, which, it appears, cannot be profitably done except on a large scale ; then often an enormous catch goes to waste for want of proper means to deal with it, and the windfall of the sea is turned into manure for the land. The new way of pickling does not seem to recommend itself to Italian tastes, for the Cornishmen are losing hold on their best market. Perhaps they have their own fault to blame : we have heard of a case where a cellarful of bad fish, condemned by the officer of health as a nuisance, was shipped off as fit food for the benighted foreigners, who keep their Popish fasts to fill British stomachs. At all events, from one cause or another, the pilchard fishery, like the Cornish mines, is not what it once was. The gigantic haul of 1833, if we are not mistaken, turned people's heads, so that all along the coast they went in for this adventure with much the same speculative spirit shown in mining; now, too many rotting boats and nets tell a tale of disappointment. But if pilchard fishery continues profitable anywhere, it is at St. Ives. Mevagissey, as we already mentioned, deals largely in that small variety known as the Cornish sardine. The real sardine, it appears, shows a disposition to fight shy of the French and Portuguese coasts; and any ill wind that kept him permanently absent there, would blow nothing but good to Cornwall, whose old toast of the three F's—"fish, tin, and copper!"—is not at present a very rousing one.

Besides pilchards, mackerel are taken in large numbers on the southern coast. Conger eels of great size, weighing from 60 to 120 lbs., are found near the shores, and among other fish should be mentioned mullet, hake, and John Dory. Readers desiring full information as to deep-sea fishing at the various points round Cornwall, may be referred to Mr. E. W. Rashleigh's *Brief Guide to Edible Cornish Fishes*, published by Mr. Wellington, Fowey.

Even when the pilchard fishery was in its prime, this did not prevent St. Ives from falling for a time behind other towns of the county, in relative position, out of which decadence it has now been revived by the railway, and by the influx of summer visitors who come in larger numbers yearly, faster than new houses can be built to accommodate them all during the height of the season. The town has a permanent nucleus of guests in the artistic colony who have settled here, after the example of the famous *Newlyn School,* near Penzance, that finds itself already surpassed in numbers. What with artists, pupils, and congenially-minded amateurs, the St. Ives School is reckoned at about one hundred strong, leavening the whole place with a flavour of tobacco, knickerbockers, and æsthetic criticism. These genial Bohemians have not altogether toned down certain Philistine prejudices of the inhabitants, but they form a friendly society among themselves, and have a snug club, including lady members of the craft, who are in force here. Models abound in the marked features of the natives, in their old-world dwellings, and in the coast scenery of the neighbourhood, which will most years be found well represented on the walls of London Exhibitions, and always in the local Art Gallery at Mr. Lanham's, close to the Market Place, who may be called the "Whiteley" of St. Ives.

The crowd of ordinary seaside visitors are expected in August and September, when the more bracing air of this side recommends it over the sheltered and relaxing south coast of Cornwall, though, indeed, the winter is seldom severe, and many constant admirers make their home or haunt here at all seasons. The frequented bathing beach is in *Porthminster Bay*, where tents and machines are used. The sands of *Porthmeor Bay* on the west, and the rocks of the Point beyond it, are preferred by men who bathe in more untrammelled fashion. Amateur sea fishing and boating are great employments ; but as for bands, balls, and other resources of sophisticated idleness, St. Ives considers itself, and rightly, to have no great need of such un-Cornish attractions. As we write, comes information of measures in view for laying out a stretch of the cliff with paths and seats, the only thing hitherto wanting to its character as a watering-place.

Our outline of the walks to be taken is in the usual order. After reconnoitring the country from an elevated point close at hand, we shall follow the railway by road back to *St. Erth*, next turn inland, and finally travel the coast in the other direction, so as to bring in several places of note not elsewhere described.

Having started our reader on these three chief roads out of St. Ives, we must remind him that he has still no idea of the number of lanes, field-paths, and moorland tracks on which he may ramble here and there till the whole neighbourhood becomes familiar. There is little danger of losing the way, unless by confusing the many engine-houses which, on the horizon, are such frequent land-marks. Guide-posts, indeed, are much to seek, it being taken for granted that every person worth considering knows the way from childhood ; but the natives, where they can be met with, are singularly courteous and ready in giving directions, while the stranger may sometimes be conferring a real favour in letting a man hear the sound of his own voice.

Those who have not time or mind for walking may see a great deal of the country by joining the Jersey Car Excursions, which start three or four times a week in the season, from the Western Hotel. Advertisements will not be wanting of the precise routes, which may vary, but a card before us promises a drive by Zennor, Gurnard's Head, and the Botallack Mine, to the Land's End and Penzance for 6s. ; another to St. Michael's Mount and Prussia Cove for 3s. 6d. ; and one all the way to the Lizard by Helston, over 25 miles, which must be called cheap at 7s. Shorter drives will, no doubt, be available, as well as occasional trips by a steam launch, which is another resource for inactive summer visitors ; and pleasure boats are to be had for rowing or sailing in the bay, beyond which inexperienced mariners will not do well to trust themselves unpiloted.

The Knill Monument.—By more than one lane behind the *Tregenna Castle Hotel,* with but little guidance but following one's eyes, one can ascend in an easy half-hour to a wind-blown wood, from the middle of which rises the queer triangular monument known as *Knill's Steeple.* This *folly* in the way of monuments, which serves as a capital land and sea mark, was built by one John Knill, a collector of customs at St. Ives in last century, who, like other local worthies, is said to have made a fortune by means that would now be held rather disreputable. He meant himself to be buried here, but going to London, and losing a great part of his property, he had to be content with a more commonplace grave. By his will, however, this eccentric character instituted a quinquennial festival to be held here, in which the vicar, the mayor, and a troupe of little girls dance solemnly round his cenotaph to the sound of fiddles. There are bequests for prizes, for a marriage portion, and for a dinner on the occasion, which may perhaps console the official personages for making themselves ridiculous. The ceremony is still carried out every five years (25th July 1896), and, like the Helston *Furry Day,* finds excuse for a good deal of revelry.

While on the head of old customs, we may mention that the almost obsolete Cornish game of "hurling" is kept up here in a ceremonial fashion. A ball to be plated with silver is used as nucleus for making a collection on the old feast day of the parish. In connection with this we observe it stated that over the door of the *Cornish Arms* inn, on the Lelant Road, may be seen fifteen silver balls on a black field, as heraldic shield of the county; but the real Cornish arms we understand to be fifteen golden bezants arranged in a triangle.

From Knill's Monument we may find our way over a rough moorland, still more broken by deserted mines, down to the little Wesleyan Chapel above *Carbis Bay,* which can most easily be reached by about a mile of the high road, leaving St. Ives at the Porthminster end, or by cliff walks rather shouldered out of the best position by the railway. From the road, at the chapel, we descend to the bay, alongside a pretty ravine. But this place belongs to our next more extended excursion.

CARBIS BAY—LELANT

TO ST. ERTH.

Carbis Bay (*Carbis Bay* Hotel and *Hendra's* Boarding-House) is a very rising dependency of St. Ives, though at present it may have a rather unfinished look. Here is a popular Pleasure-Ground of the place-to-spend-a-happy-day order, with swings, roundabouts, and such like, much in favour with excursionists from the mining districts; but we understand that this feature is likely to be removed before long, so as to let Carbis Bay fulfil its destiny as a quiet family watering-place. The hotel stands on the shore at the bottom of the gorge, and new lodging-houses are springing up above the fine beach of sand. The boarding-house here is spoken of as remarkably comfortable for the moderation of its terms, so that it is not deserted even in winter. The hotel is new, and seems likely to be successful. St. Ives is only a mile away, to which Carbis Bay will soon be linked by a chain of airy villas. Between the latter and *Lelant* are the Golf-Links, where many of the St. Ives people and other neighbours have taken the prevailing epidemic in a severe form.

Hawke's Point, the headland beyond Carbis Bay, is another site of tea-gardens, a great place for picnics, with a Wishing Well, in which many crooked pins are dropped, and if the unspoken wish be a pleasant day's outing, it will often be fulfilled. A path leads to the embowered Grotto at the top, where there is a fine view over Hayle Harbour.

The road, soon turning up this estuary, in about 3 miles from St. Ives, comes to **Lelant**, one of those parishes that have had much ado to save themselves from the sand, now turned to profitable account as excellent golf-links. There is an inn here, and lodgings can be found by golfers and artists. The church of *St. Uny*, some way from the village, has interesting features in the remains of Norman arching, rare hereabouts, and a fine pointed arch of the 15th century, besides a curious font and dial. We find an old cross in the churchyard, and several others to be sought out within the bounds of the parish. Behind it are the woods of *Trevethoe*, over which rises *Trecrobben* or *Trencom* Hill (550 feet), with an ancient castle on the top and some fine rock scenery, which have suggested legends of giants' handiwork. A climb here is well worth making for the view of both coasts; and thence, or by the road, we come down to the ancient bridge at St. Erth. From *Lelant* the Hayle River may be crossed by a causeway bridge towards St. Erth, or by ferry-boat to the *Weir*, whence is reached the quarter of Hayle known as *Copperhouse.*

St. Erth is a large village, lying to the east of the railway, with a well-restored church and a pretty churchyard. An ancient cross may be found where one would hardly expect to see such a relic of popery, in the yard of a dissenting chapel. There are ironworks here, once used for copper. A little way up the river are the avenue and manor house of *Trewinnard*, now a farm, but containing some old tapestry, and a curious specimen of a family coach, preserved from early days of such conveyances. Two Roman camps can be traced in this parish.

TO PENZANCE BY CASTLE-AN-DINAS.

The road just described is that usually taken in driving to *Penzance*, for, though it adds a mile or two to the distance, its ascent is not so trying as on the old road cutting right across the central heights of the peninsula, which should be preferred for walking. This road (8 m.) leaves the back of St. Ives by the valley called the *Stennack*, but visitors at the Tregenna Castle Hotel, or the Porthminster end, can gain it by following the lane which goes off opposite Porthminster House, soon doubling back to the left, to pass between the *Tennis Club Ground* and the park of Tregenna. When one has got almost to the latitude of Knill's Steeple on the left, a path and stiles must be taken across the fields to the right, which will bring one into *Halsetown*, that bears a curious resemblance to a toy village spread out on the hill-side by some giant's child. Bearing through this, a little to the right, one strikes the old Penzance road. Upward it runs over wild moorlands, by boulders and smokeless engine shafts. Over the ridge we descend through the scattered hamlets of *Nancledrea*, which, with its three taverns, looks as if, like the mines around, it had seen better days. Beyond the brook, at the bottom, the ground again rises, swelling up to the height of about 750 feet, where stands the beacon tower of **Castle-an-Dinas**, an old British fortification (*Endennis* on some maps). The road passes this on its right about half-way to Penzance, but leisurely travellers might well ascend for a view over the whole peninsula and the sea on each side. It is said that two dozen parish churches can be seen from this point. A mile or so to the west of it would be found the fortified British village of *Chysauster*, remains of much antiquarian interest. If we hold on by the road, it drops down upon a fine prospect of Mount's Bay to *Gulval,* where, opposite the churchyard gate, a broad field path will carry us to the road from Marazion, just outside of Penzance, soon reaching the railway station, from which a return might be made (10 m.) through *St. Erth Junction;* or, to the left, *Marazion Road Station* is under 2 miles from Gulval.

TO TOWEDNACK, ZENNOR, GURNARD'S HEAD, ETC.

The road westward does not at first keep very near the coast, but, at first identical with the old road to Penzance, goes out by the *Stennack,* past the Western Hotel, and up the valley behind the town. A lane to the right is marked as leading to *Clodgy,* the first headland beyond St. Ives, for which it gathers up other ways rising from the cemetery at the base of the Island, and through the new houses on the west of the valley. From *Clodgy Point,* the enterprising tourist could, no doubt, make his way, by hook or crook, not far from the shore, but in dirty weather this route is hardly to be recommended.

On the high road our guide will be the town lamps, which, as is the custom with frugal Cornish communities, are extinguished betimes, unless when and where they can serve as beacons to the fishermen. Passing the "New Church" of *Halsetown,* to the right, at a blacksmith's shop, the road divides, left for Penzance, right for Zennor. Above this point rises the rugged *Rosewall Hill,* suggesting nothing so little as roses. The name is that of an old local family, perhaps derived from a Celtic word for heath.

Behind this height lies **Towednack** church town, a short 3 miles from St. Ives, to be reached either by turning almost at once to the right from the *Penzance* Road, beyond the parting just mentioned, or by taking a short turn to the left from the *Zennor Road,* more than a mile on, where it makes a wide bend inland. The low church of *Towednack* is not likely to be confused with the tall engine houses that dominate it. The absence of pinnacles on this tower is accounted for by the persistent hostility of a certain ghostly enemy very active in Cornish legends. The church has no other feature to catch the ordinary tourist's attention, but an architect would find some points of interest, in the tower staircase, for instance, and the early chancel arch.

In the give-and-take of well-worn jokes which tickles rustic wit, the Towednack people are said to have built a wall round the cuckoo, to which they retort on St. Ives men, "Who whipped the hake?"—whereby hangs a tale—and hurl back scorn for scorn on Zennor, as the place where "the cow ate the bell rope," the sting of which probably is that she could get nothing better to eat. Gotham always is the next parish, or in the next county, as here "Lincolnshire Yellow bellies" or "Wiltshire Moon rakers" are paralleled by "St. Ives Hakes" and "Towednack Cuckoos."

The church tower points to a path which will lead us on to the moor beside a quarry, whose granite is about to see life in the new harbour of Mevagissey. Behind rises a ridge, crowned by what in Devon would be called *tors*, one of which, known under two or three names, *Trendrine Hill* in the Ordnance Survey map, is about 800 feet high, and looks out as far as the Scillies in clear weather. Over these heights we come down again on the Zennor Road, which, after taking a wide curve inland, mounts again to pass behind the *Eagle's Nest*, easily recognised by its prominent situation, and by its being the only elegant house in a stony neighbourhood, which one local guide book aptly compares to Connemara, while a Crimean veteran, whose lot is to live here, has been strongly reminded of the Balaclava valley of death, but he admits with a sigh the likeness to Irish wilds for uncongenial solitude. Instead of eating the bell rope, however, that cow would have done well to stray afield on the strip of plain reaching down to the sea, where farms are seen making shift to flourish below the moorland heights.

From the Eagle's Nest, the road again dips downward, and round the next turn we come in sight of **Zennor** (5 m.), the way to which might or might not have been abridged by trying to cut straighter across country. Here we find an inn and a restored 15th-century church, containing an ancient font and a curious carved bench end, representing a mermaid, which has its legend of an unhappy youth seduced by a sea maiden, as so often happened in the good old times. Zennor would hardly hold up its head as a true Cornish parish without some fragment of an old cross, and one accordingly is to be seen here. Some way from the church is a logan-stone, and, on the hill above, *Zennor Quoit*, said to be the largest cromlech in the country, if not in Europe.

ST. GURNARD'S HEAD

Some 2 miles more brings us to **Gurnard's Head**, the grandest piece of rock scenery within the St. Ives district. The driving road must be left at the village of *Trereen*, and the fields crossed for half a mile to the promontory, with its stern caves and cliffs. On the neck are the remains of a chapel, and the head beyond, as denoted by the old name *Trereen Dinas*, was once adapted as one of the fortresses so common along this coast. There is an inn at Trereen, and another which calls itself the *Gurnard's Head Hotel*, with as little of the hotel about it as may be but the charges.

We have now come a good way from St. Ives, but, while we are about it, may as well push on about as far to cover a stretch of coast which may not be reached from Penzance. The next parish is *Morvah*, and as we advance towards the Land's End, the scenery seems to grow more wild, more desolate, more truly Cornish, like the stump of a cigar gathering up the dregs of its flavour. Our local guide is very amusing about the parish patriotism of these regions, known as the "high countries." They are, or were, it seems, Cornishmen of the most Cornish, like the inhabitants of *la Bretagne bretonnante*, over the Channel. "Natives of these places once considered themselves vastly superior to the inhabitants of St. Ives and Lelant, and every bare-legged infant thanked the goodness and the grace that made him a happy Zennor, Morvah, or Towednack child. But the times are altered now; tea and slops have supplanted the old-fashioned wholesome country diet, flimsy hats and dresses have taken the place of comfortable homespuns, country dances are condemned as not sufficiently genteel, the fiddler is extinct, and quadrilles and polkas are politely warbled by the popular though execrable concertina. However, much of the 'auld warld' still lingers in the high countries. Visitors will here perhaps see, for the first time, the immense open chimney, with dried furze and peat-turf piled up on the earthen floor of the kitchen." This, indeed, was written some dozen years ago, and there is no saying what fresh innovations may have come in the wake of school boards and county councils. The population appears not to have increased; too many tumble-down empty cottages tell their tale of mining misfortune. It was somewhere in this neighbourhood that an enterprising artist and his wife led a Robinson Crusoe existence in an abandoned engine-house.

Once upon a time this region must have been relatively more populous, its natural fastnesses recommending it to our British forefathers for securing Home Rule against Saxon or other intruders. Did one keep to the heights, he could come to *St. Just* by a line thickly studded with antiquities, cairns, barrows, cromlechs, camps, and ancient settlements, the most remarkable of which, perhaps, are the singularly preserved beehive huts of **Bosporthennis,** between *Trereen* and *Mulfra Hill,* with its *Quoit* or *Cromlech;* then behind *Morvah,* **Chun** *Castle* and *Cromlech,* the former one of the best specimens of a circular camp. We do not attempt to go into further detail, as readers capable of taking interest in these remains are like to be provided with better guidance, such as Mr. Borlase's *Nœnia Cornubiæ.* There is a Penzance Guide by the Rev. W. S. Lach-Szyrma, which gives a full list of the antiquarian points in Penwith.

If we lengthened our walk by hugging the shore, we should still have a fine stretch of cliffs and coves, of which the most prominent feature is *Bosigran Head,* site of another cliff castle, and of a logan-stone. Below *Carn Galver,* to the left, the highest land hereabouts, by moors and mines and hamlets not worth naming to be forgotten, the road leads us on to **Morvah,** of note only as church town of a scattered parish. Hence it is a mile or two to **Pendeen,** that has two inns and some sights to show, besides its cove and headland, in the artificial cavern of *Pendeen Van,* apparently a subterranean place of concealment, such as are met with elsewhere in the county—in the old manor-house of *Pendeen,* now a farm, the birthplace of Dr. *Borlase,* the antiquary, —and in the modern church, built by the Rev. R. Aitken, the well-known revivalist, as an imitation of Iona Cathedral, containing memorials to him, a fine reredos, and painted glass.

One more bend of this coast let us take here, though it might be more conveniently explored from *St. Just,* lying a mile behind the farther end. We soon come to the *Levant Mine,* one of the few Cornish copper mines that, at the date of writing, seem to be doing not badly. A little farther on is the more famous **Botallack,** over which is now written *Ichabod.* Yet still, this submarine mine forms an extraordinary scene, bespeaking man's bold dealings with nature. The extreme depth is 1050 feet, and some of the galleries stretch hundreds of feet under the ocean-bed. The roar of the sea was sometimes so terrific that even the stout hearts of the miners would fail them when working the submarine galleries. The descent used to be one of the features of a Cornish tour, but this mine is not at present in a state to be visited.

The next bold projection is *Kenidjack Castle*, then we come round to **Cape Cornwall** (230 feet), which, from its commanding attitude, seems worthier to be the farthest point of England than the *Land's End*, now full in view, and soon to be visited from the other side of this peninsula.

Andrew Gill: I have collected historical photographs and optical antiques for over forty years. I am a professional 'magic lantern' showman presenting Victorian slide shows and giving talks on early optical entertainments for museums, festivals, special interest groups and universities. Please visit my website **'Magic Lantern World'** at www.magiclanternist.com

My booklets and photo albums are available from Amazon, simply search for the titles below. If you've enjoyed this book, please leave a review on Amazon, as good ratings are very important to independent authors. If you're disappointed, please let me know the reason, so that I can address the issue in future editions.

Historical travel guides
New York
Jersey in 1921
Norwich in 1880
Doon the Watter
Liverpool in 1886
Nottingham in 1899
Bournemouth in 1914
Great Yarmouth in 1880
Victorian Walks in Surrey
The Way We Were: Bath
A Victorian Visit to Brighton
The Way We Were: Lincoln
A Victorian Visit to Hastings
A Victorian Visit to Falmouth
Newcastle upon Tyne in 1903
Victorian and Edwardian York
The Way We Were: Llandudno
A Victorian Visit to North Devon
The Way We Were: Manchester
A Victorian Guide to Birmingham
Leeds through the Magic Lantern
An Edwardian Guide to Leicester
Victorian and Edwardian Bradford
Victorian and Edwardian Sheffield

The Way We Were: North Cornwall
A Victorian Visit to Fowey and Looe
A Victorian Visit to Peel, Isle of Man
Doncaster through the Magic Lantern
The Way We Were: The Lake District
Lechlade to Oxford by Canoe in 1875
Guernsey, Sark and Alderney in 1921
East Devon through the Magic Lantern
The River Thames from Source to Sea
A Victorian Visit to Ramsey, Isle of Man
A Victorian Visit to Douglas, Isle of Man
Victorian Totnes through the Magic Lantern
Victorian Whitby through the Magic Lantern
Victorian London through the Magic Lantern
St. Ives through the Victorian Magic Lantern
Victorian Torquay through the Magic Lantern
Victorian Glasgow through the Magic Lantern
The Way We Were: Wakefield and Dewsbury
The Way We Were: Hebden Bridge to Halifax
Victorian Blackpool through the Magic Lantern
Victorian Scarborough through the Magic Lantern
The Way We Were: Hull and the Surrounding Area
The Way We Were: Harrogate and Knaresborough
A Victorian Tour of North Wales: Rhyl to Llandudno
A Victorian Visit to Lewes and the surrounding area
The Isle of Man through the Victorian Magic Lantern
A Victorian Visit to Helston and the Lizard Peninsula
A Victorian Railway Journey from Plymouth to Padstow
A Victorian Visit to Barmouth and the Surrounding Area
The Way We Were: Holmfirth, Honley and Huddersfield
A Victorian Visit to Malton, Pickering and Castle Howard
A Victorian Visit to Eastbourne and the surrounding area
A Victorian Visit to Aberystwyth and the Surrounding Area
The Way We Were: Rotherham and the Surrounding Area
A Victorian Visit to Castletown, Port St. Mary and Port Erin
Penzance and Newlyn through the Victorian Magic Lantern
A Victorian Journey to Snowdonia, Caernarfon and Pwllheli
Victorian Brixham and Dartmouth through the Magic Lantern
Victorian Plymouth and Devonport through the Magic Lantern
A Victorian Tour of North Wales: Conwy to Caernarfon via Anglesey
Staithes, Runswick and Robin Hood's Bay through the Magic Lantern
Dawlish, Teignmouth and Newton Abbot through the Victorian Magic Lantern

Walking Books
Victorian Edinburgh Walks
Victorian Rossendale Walks
More Victorian Rossendale Walks
Victorian Walks on the Isle of Wight (Book 1)

Victorian Walks on the Isle of Wight (Book 2)
Victorian Rossendale Walks: The End of an Era

Other historical topics
The YMCA in the First World War
Sarah Jane's Victorian Tour of Scotland
The River Tyne through the Magic Lantern
The 1907 Wrench Cinematograph Catalogue
Victorian Street Life through the Magic Lantern
The First World War through the Magic Lantern
Ballyclare May Fair through the Victorian Magic Lantern
The Story of Burnley's Trams through the Magic Lantern
The Franco-British 'White City' London Exhibition of 1908
The 1907 Wrench 'Optical and Science Lanterns' Catalogue
The CWS Crumpsall Biscuit Factory through the Magic Lantern
How They Built the Forth Railway Bridge: A Victorian Magic Lantern Show

Historical photo albums (just photos)
The Way We Were: Suffolk
Norwich: The Way We Were
The Way We Were: Somerset
Fife through the Magic Lantern
York through the Magic Lantern
Rossendale: The Way We Were
The Way We Were: Cumberland
Burnley through the Magic Lantern
Oban to the Hebrides and St. Kilda
Tasmania through the Magic Lantern
Swaledale through the Magic Lantern
Llandudno through the Magic Lantern
Birmingham through the Magic Lantern
Penzance, Newlyn and the Isles of Scilly
Great Yarmouth through the Magic Lantern
Ancient Baalbec through the Magic Lantern
The Isle of Skye through the Magic Lantern
Ancient Palmyra through the Magic Lantern
The Kentish Coast from Whitstable to Hythe
New South Wales through the Magic Lantern
From Glasgow to Rothesay by Paddle Steamer
Victorian Childhood through the Magic Lantern
The Way We Were: Yorkshire Railway Stations
Southampton, Portsmouth and the Great Liners
Newcastle upon Tyne through the Magic Lantern
Egypt's Ancient Monuments through the Magic Lantern
The Way We Were: Birkenhead, Port Sunlight and the Wirral
Ancient Egypt, Baalbec and Palmyra through the Magic Lantern

Contact email: victorianhistory@virginmedia.com

Printed in Great Britain
by Amazon

74144457R00037